SPACE,
INCORPORATED

THE FUTURE OF COMMERCIAL
SPACE TRAVEL

TAMRA B. ORR

CONTENT CONSULTANT
SARAH RUIZ
Aerospace Engineer

CAPSTONE PRESS
a capstone imprint

Edge Books are published by Capstone Press,
1710 Roe Crest Drive, North Mankato, Minnesota 56003
www.capstonepub.com

Library of Congress Cataloging-in-Publication Data
Names: Orr, Tamra, author.
Title: Space, incorporated : the future of commercial space travel / by Tamra B. Orr.
Description: North Nankato, MN : Capstone Press, [2019] | Series: Edge books.
Future space | Audience: Age 10. | Audience: Grades 4 to 6. | Includes bibliographical references
and index.
Identifiers: LCCN 2019003346 (print) | LCCN 2019010351 (ebook)
ISBN 9781543572742 (eBook PDF) | ISBN 9781543572667 (library binding)
ISBN 9781543575200 (pbk.)
Subjects: LCSH: Space tourism—Juvenile literature. | Space industrialization—Juvenile literature.
| Outer space—Civilian use—Juvenile literature. | Outer space—Exploration—Juvenile
literature. Classification: LCC TL793 (ebook) | LCC TL793 .077 2019 (print) | DDC 338.0999—dc23
LC record available at https://lccn.loc.gov/2019003346

Editorial Credits
Mandy Robbins, editor; Laura Mitchell, designer; Jo Miller, media researcher;
Katy LaVigne, production specialist

Image Credits
NASA, 5, 8, 10, 11; Newscom: Cover Images/Stratolaunch Systems Corp., 29, MEGA/EM, 28, Science
Photo Library, 12, TNS/Red Huber, 12, ZUMA Press/Chris Meaney, 25, ZUMA Press/Virgin Galactic,
22–23; Shutterstock: Everett Historical, 7; Wikimedia: NASA, Cover, 26, 27, NASA/JSC/Robert
Markowitz, 20–21, SpaceX, 17, 18

Design Elements
Capstone; Shutterstock: Audrius Birbilas

All internet sites appearing in back matter were available and accurate when this book was sent to
press.

Printed and bound in the United States of America.
PA70

TABLE OF CONTENTS

CHAPTER ONE

BLASTING INTO SPACE

Imagine you could buy a ticket, hop on a spaceship, and blast off into space. For years, authors and movie-makers have imagined a future where space travel is fast, fun, and fabulous. So far, though, only professionally trained astronauts or incredibly wealthy travelers have been able to travel into space. A few have even visited the **International Space Station** (ISS).

SPACE FACT:

One thing the first space tourists will not be able to do is visit the restroom. Most of the early vehicles will not include bathrooms!

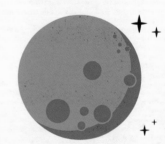

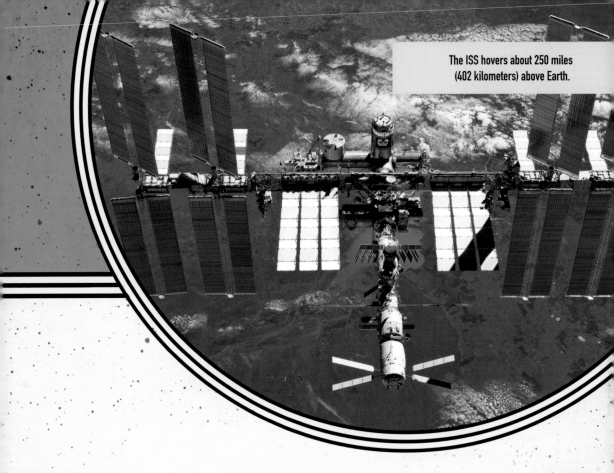

The ISS hovers about 250 miles (402 kilometers) above Earth.

That may not be true for much longer. Thanks to private companies such as SpaceX and Blue Origin, space tourism may happen sooner than once thought. The first trips will be less than an hour, but during that time passengers will experience **weightlessness** and see the most amazing images of the Earth passing below.

International Space Station—a place for astronauts to live and work in space

weightlessness—a state in which a person feels free of the pull of Earth's gravity

A BRIEF HISTORY OF SPACE FLIGHT

The journey from looking up at the stars to flying toward them has been a long one. The first long-distance rockets were invented not for exploring, but for bombing. During World War II (1939–1945), these missiles bombed major cities in Europe. The former Soviet Union used that same rocket technology to launch its first artificial **satellite** in 1957.

The Soviets' success in space flight spurred the United States to shift its focus to getting Americans into space. The U.S. government created the National Aeronautics and Space Administration (NASA) with the goal of getting Americans into space before the Soviets. This time period was called "the space race." By 1962, American astronaut John Glenn had circled Earth in a spacecraft. In 1969, Neil Armstrong walked on the moon. Between 1969 and 1972, NASA sent six Apollo missions to explore the moon. By 1980, their spacecraft had taken photos of Jupiter, Mars, Venus, Mercury, and Saturn.

satellite—an object in space that circles a larger object, such as a planet; artificial satellites send signals and information from one place to another

A U.S. rocket based on German missiles
from World War II blasts off in 1950.

The space shuttle Columbia launched on April 12, 1981.

FROM SHUTTLES TO THE ISS

In the 1980s, the U.S. began using **space shuttles** to travel to and from space. But in 1986, the 25th shuttle exploded, killing all on board. In 2003, another shuttle lost control and broke apart on its way back to Earth. The space shuttle program launched 135 missions. It was ended in 2011, however, due in part to the catastrophes. But it was also because NASA was shifting its focus, money, and energy to maintaining the ISS.

Organizations such as NASA, the European Space Agency, Canadian Space Agency, and Japanese Aerospace Exploration Agency (JAXA), continue to explore the possibilities of space. Now private companies have joined them. Thanks to developments in technology, many companies are able to build rockets—and do it for less money than governments can. One day these private companies just might make flying to Mars as common as flying across the country on vacation.

The Dragon

Astronauts from many countries, including the United States, Russia, Japan, Italy, and Canada, have worked in the ISS since 2000. When the ISS needs supplies, SpaceX's Dragon is one of four vehicles that come to the rescue. In six years, the Dragon has made 16 unmanned trips to the ISS. It has brought everything from equipment and computer hardware to food, water, and other basic living supplies.

space shuttle—a spacecraft that is meant to carry astronauts into space and back to Earth

CHAPTER TWO

WHY GO TO SPACE?

Flying into space costs a great deal of money. It uses up resources. It takes huge amounts of time and effort. So why explore space in the first place? What could humanity gain by exploring outer space? There has to be more to it than just taking an out-of-this-world vacation.

SPACE FACT:

Inventions for space missions have improved life on Earth. They include hand-held vacuums and freeze-dried foods.

Astronauts at the ISS depend on deliveries from Earth for their basic necessities.

SUPPORTING THE ISS

Currently, it's important to return to space to support the astronauts living on the ISS. They depend on these missions for supplies and transportation to and from Earth. While they are on the ISS, the astronauts conduct important experiments that impact life on Earth. They also learn information about space that could benefit humanity now and in the future.

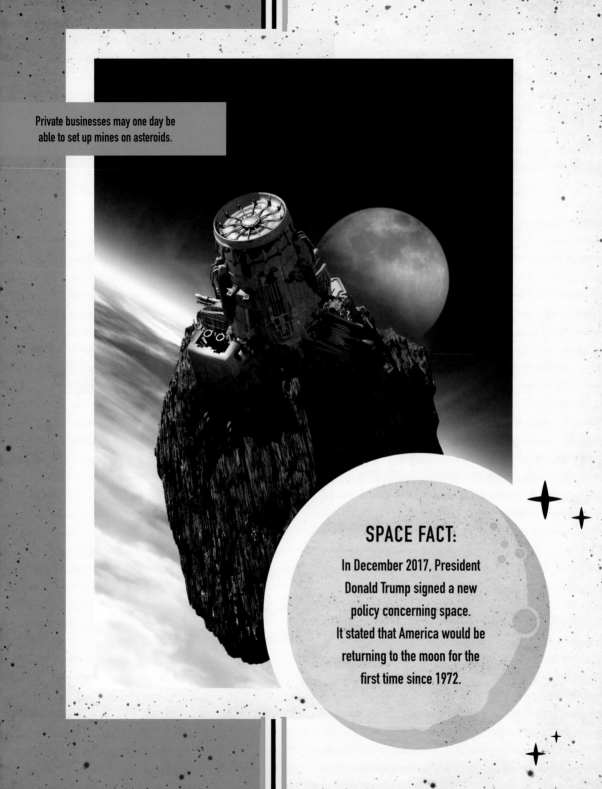

Private businesses may one day be able to set up mines on asteroids.

SPACE FACT:

In December 2017, President Donald Trump signed a new policy concerning space. It stated that America would be returning to the moon for the first time since 1972.

MAKING MONEY IN SPACE

Private companies see exciting money-making possibilities in space. Space tourism is only one of them. Many companies also want to go to space to mine valuable metals such as gold, silver, and platinum. While some minerals are found on **asteroids**, others are found as close as the moon. A rare metal called tantalum is there. It is used in various types of electronics and solar panels.

SAVING HUMANITY

Some experts believe that developing a space program is the key to protecting Earth. For example, if a large asteroid is heading our way, a spacecraft could be launched to knock the asteroid off course.

Space exploration could even save all of humanity. If planet Earth ever becomes unable to support human life, people will need somewhere to go. For example, if Earth's climate changes too drastically, a new planet to call home might be the only solution for humanity's survival.

asteroid—a large space rock that moves around the Sun; asteroids are too small to be called planets

CHAPTER THREE

GOING PRIVATE: A NEW KIND OF SPACE RACE

Space flight changed dramatically in 2004. In the United States, Congress passed a policy encouraging private companies to develop their own rockets and vehicles. Up until then, governments were mostly responsible for the technology, equipment, and high costs of space exploration.

It did not take long for many companies and their billionaire CEOs to make plans for blasting off into space. Elon Musk developed SpaceX. Jeff Bezos, owner of Amazon, created Blue Origin. Britain's Sir Richard Branson founded Virgin Galactic. People also started new companies all around the world. They include iSpace in China, PD Aerospace in Japan, and Zero 2 Infinity in Spain.

There are even a few small private space programs. Copenhagen Suborbitals in Denmark has been building and flying rockets since 2011. They are entirely supported by donations from their followers.

SPACE FACT:

In August 2018, Copenhagen Suborbitals launched the unmanned Nexø II rocket. It reached the edge of Earth's atmosphere. Their next goal is to launch the Spica rocket. It will be a manned flight.

RECYCLED ROCKETS

Private companies are able to launch rockets at much less cost than previous government launches. One reason why is because they have made advancements in reusable rockets. In the past, most rockets were destroyed or lost during a mission to space. Many rocket parts from NASA launches fell into the sea. Some, such as the shuttle rocket boosters, were recovered, repaired, and used again. Other parts are still sitting on the bottom of the oceans.

Reusable rockets have changed the business of launching rockets. They are designed to go to space and then return to Earth to be used again. It has taken years to develop the technology needed for these rockets. SpaceX spent $1 billion over 15 years before inventing a successful and reliable one. Now many companies have a version of this technology.

SpaceX's Falcon Heavy rocket has many reusable stages. As of 2019, the rocket had eight missions planned.

The Falcon 9's fins help stabilize it for a controlled landing.

LAUNCHING ROCKETS

All rockets launch in several stages. Each stage propels the rocket to a certain height and then falls away from the spacecraft. With each stage, the spacecraft is launched higher, until it reaches space. Previously, once these rockets fell away, they could never be used again.

Reusable rockets are made differently than traditional rockets. Take Space X's Falcon 9 rocket, for example. The first stage propels the rocket to the edge of space. Then it separates from the spacecraft, flips over, and returns to Earth. Unlike traditional rockets that only have enough fuel to reach space, reusable rockets have extra fuel. This fuel allows the rocket to control its return to Earth, rather than just falling back to the surface. The extra fuel also allows the engines to control the rocket's speed.

The rocket has "fins" built into the sides. They pop out as the rocket comes down. These fins help steer the rocket so that it lands on the landing pad.

THE COMMERCIAL CREW PROGRAM

How might reusable rockets be used on future missions? They may be part of NASA's Commercial Crew Program. Its main goal is to transport crew members and equipment to and from the ISS. The vehicles used for this program could also be used to **evacuate** the ISS crew in an emergency.

NASA chose to work with SpaceX and Boeing on this project. The two companies have been working hard to create spacecraft for the job. One is the SpaceX Crew Dragon, that currently supplies the ISS with deliveries.

The astronauts who will fly on the Starliner and Crew Dragon pose in front of the spacecraft.

The other is Boeing's CST-100 Starliner. It has a built-in airbag and parachute to allow it to land on the ground. The Starliner can be used up to 10 times.

The first of the Commercial Crew Program's flights will be unmanned. However, plans are underway for both companies to send up manned flights. Nine astronauts are scheduled to go on the first Boeing Starliner and SpaceX Crew Dragon missions.

evacuate—to move people to safety from a dangerous place

VACATION IN SPACE?

Reusable rockets will also make space tourism more possible and affordable. Virgin Galactic's rocket-powered plane VSS Unity will take space tourists to the edge of space for $250,000 per person. That's still a lot of money. But it's a lot less than the $58 million dollars it currently costs for a trip to the ISS. To launch the Unity, the spacecraft hitches a ride on an airplane. Then it takes off from a platform on the airplane and uses its reusable rocket engine to propel it into space.

The VSS Unity launches from the middle platform of an aircraft called the WhiteKnightTwo. It looks like two airplanes joined by the center wings.

In 2018, VSS Unity was still being tested. But that December, it successfully reached space for the first time. The event marked the first successful manned space flight from U.S. soil since NASA's space shuttle program ended in 2011. Two pilots flew the VSS Unity to the edge of space, as defined by the U.S. Air Force. It went about 50 miles (80.5 km) above Earth's surface. Virgin Galactic's founder, Richard Branson, called it, "our biggest dream and our toughest challenge."

SPACE FACT:

The VSS Enterprise was an earlier Virgin rocket-powered plane. It crashed, killing the pilot on a test flight.

CHASING ASTEROIDS

Some of the commercial spacecraft being launched are not going to planets or moons. Instead, they have other destinations. In 2016, NASA launched the OSIRIS-REx. The private company Lockheed Martin Space System built this research spacecraft to fly to the asteroid Bennu. Researchers at the University of Arizona will study the information and samples obtained by OSIRIS-REx. Their goal is to learn about the formation of our **solar system** and possibly even the origins of life on Earth.

In late 2018, OSIRIS-REx got close enough to start taking photographs of the skyscraper-sized asteroid. It will keep taking photos until it can create a 3-D map of the asteroid's surface. In addition, the spacecraft uses its on-board equipment to analyze the chemicals found on the asteroid. Soon it will use its robotic arm to reach out and take a small sample from Bennu. That sample will return to Earth in 2023 for researchers at the University of Arizona to study.

solar system—the Sun and all the planets, moons, comets, and smaller bodies orbiting it

an artist's illustration of OSIRIS-REx approaching the asteroid Bennu

25

CHAPTER FOUR

THE FUTURE OF SPACE TOURISM

As launching into space becomes less expensive, more people will jump at the chance to leave Earth. NASA plans to create an outpost in space near the moon called Gateway in the 2020s. SpaceX owner Elon Musk believes he will step foot on—and even **colonize**—Mars during his lifetime.

Dennis Tito (left) with Russian crewmates on the ISS

The World's First Space Tourist

In April 2001, Dennis Tito's dream came true. For about $20 million, Tito rode in the Russian Soyuz rocket and spent eight days on the ISS. He circled the Earth 128 times. At least six people have followed Tito. Each time, the price tag has gone up. The last private citizen to fly to space was Guy Laliberte. His ticket was $35 million!

Before humans can successfully set foot on Mars, they will have to solve some problems related to space travel. One of the problems is how to carry enough fuel on board to complete a mission and get back home. NASA is looking into installing a number of **propellant** depots in space. Like a gas station, these depots would offer the fuel needed to fill up a spacecraft when it gets low.

colonize—to send people to live in a new land or another planet
propellant—fuel that is burned to give thrust or power to a rocket

The first space hotel, Orion Span, could be open to guests as soon as 2022.

SPACE FACT:

Experts worry about **radiation** in deep space. StemRad is a company that is working on a protective vest.
If it tests well, the vest could be standard equipment for use in deep space.

radiation—dangerous energy emitted as rays, electromagnetic waves, or particles

SPACE HOTELS?

If space travel becomes more common, it will likely attract some of the world's wealthiest tourists. In that case, space hospitality becomes a brand new business. Will the closest planets or moons end up with coffee shops, hotels, and restaurants? It is possible. A company called Orion Span announced in 2018 that it plans to build the world's first luxury space hotel that will orbit Earth. Construction is scheduled to start in 2021. The company even plans to build condos in case people want to stay more than a few days.

Few people get the chance to look at Earth from outer space. However, if space travel becomes easier and less expensive, tickets to space may become possible for more people.

Airplane to the Stars

The Stratolaunch is the largest plane ever built. Its wingspan is longer than a football field. It looks like two planes connected in the middle. It takes off from a runway, but at 35,000 feet (10,668 meters), one or more shuttle vehicles will be released. They will carry cargo, and someday maybe passengers, off to other parts of space.

GLOSSARY

asteroid (AS-tuh-royd)—a large space rock that moves around the Sun; asteroids are too small to be called planets

colonize (KAH-luh-nyz)—to send people to live in a new land or another planet

evacuate (i-VA-kyuh-wayt)—to move people to safety from a dangerous place

International Space Station (in-tur-NASH-uh-nuhl SPAYSS STAY-shuhn)—a place for astronauts to live and work in space

propellant (pruh-PEL-uhnt)—fuel that is burned to give thrust or power to a rocket

radiation (ray-dee-AY-shuhn)—dangerous energy emitted as rays, electromagnetic waves, or particles

satellite (SAT-uh-lite)—an object that moves around a planet or other cosmic body; often a spacecraft used to send signals and information from one place to another

solar system (SOH-lur SISS-tuhm)—the sun and all the planets, moons, comets, and smaller bodies orbiting it

space shuttle (SPAYSS SHUHT-uhl)—a spacecraft that is meant to carry astronauts into space and back to Earth

weightlessness (WAIT-less-ness)—a state in which a person feels free of the pull of Earth's gravity

READ MORE

Mahoney, Emily. *How Will People Travel to Mars?* Space Mysteries. New York: Gareth Stevens Publishing, 2018.

Mara, Wil. *Breakthroughs in Space Travel.* Space Exploration. Minneapolis: Lerner Publications, 2019.

Spilsbury, Richard. *Space.* Adventures in STEAM. North Mankato, MN: Capstone Press, 2019.

INTERNET SITES

Easy Science for Kids
https://easyscienceforkids.com/all-about-space-travel/

Kids Astronomy
https://kidsastronomy.com/space-exploration/

Our Universe for Kids
https://www.ouruniverseforkids.com/spacetravel/

INDEX